THE SECRET ART OF
DEROBIO ESCRIMA

THE SECRET ART OF DEROBIO ESCRIMA

A Martial Art of the Philippines

DAN MEDINA

www.TambuliMedia.com
Spring House, PA USA

DISCLAIMER

The author and publisher of this book DISCLAIM ANY RESPONSIBILITY over any in-jury as a result of the techniques taught in this book. The reader is advised to consult a physician as to his physical condition to assume any strenuous training or dangerous physical activity. This is a martial arts book and trains dangerous techniques that can cause serious physical injury and even death. Practice and training requires a fit and healthy student and a qualified instructor.

We do not offer any legal advice. Any statement which may be interpreted as a legal advice is pure opinion of the author and has no basis in law. He is not a US trained lawyer. In the event of any incident using your training as a martial artist, exercise your Miranda Rights. Remain silent and consult your attorney before you say anything to the cops or the people around you. Any self-incriminating statements uttered by you will be used against you in court.

Copyright ©2014 Dan Medina

ISBN-13: 978-0692331538 (Tambuli Media)
ISBN-10: 0692331530

Edited by Mark V. Wiley
Cover by Stephanie Medina
Design by Summer Bonne

The Escrimador's Creed

An escrimador must have the wisdom and discretion to know when to use his or her art.

When forced to use it, he or she must show humanity against aggressors who cannot defend against it and the humbleness not to boast about the power he or she holds.

In doing so, he or she will gain harmony both with their art and their lives.

—Great Grandmaster Braulio Pedoy

ACKNOWLEDGMENTS

There are many whom I would like to thank, and without whose help and inspiration, this book would not have been possible.

First, thank you to my wife and love of my life, Stephanie Medina. Her unyielding support, encouragement and long hours of photo editing were instrumental in being able to make this project go from concept to reality.

To my son, Steven Colby, and my brother-in-law, Eric Fenzl, for adding the much needed flair to my words.

To my students who dedicated many weekends to posing for the photo sequences in this book: my son Michael Colby, Shane Friendly, Logan Peck, Mike Kilpatrick, and Mike Wanke.

A special thank you to Tuhon Brandon Jordan, who was always there telling me that I needed to tell the world about Derobio Escrima and for being there by my side as I did.

Thank you Master Antionette Chavez for supporting me and representing the art in New Mexico.

Thank you, Professor Melchor Chavez, Arjan Arlan Sanford, and Michael Wanke for inspiring me as students and for continuing to inspire as Masters of Derobio

Thank you to Sr. Master Carlton Kramer, Tuhon Chaz Siangco, and Sr. Master Ron England for providing historical photos for this book.

A special thank you to GM Dr. Mark Wiley and Tambuli Media for giving me the opportunity to write this book.

My greatest thank you goes to Great Grand-Master Braulio Tomada Pedoy and his son Batikan Eduardo James Pedoy for unselfishly sharing this art and its secrets with me.

Photo Credit: Steve R. Leimberg

Thank you, all.

—Grandmaster Dan Medina
Kingsland, Georgia 2014

FOREWORD

The martial arts of the Philippines are so vast and varied, one cannot count them all. It is impossible. Why? Because unlike the martial arts of Japan, Okinawa and China, Filipino martial artists have not placed much emphasis on lineage. That is to say, keeping record of their actual teachers, their teacher's teachers and so on; nor maintaining the name of the style through the generations. Indeed, because the Filipino martial arts are in a constant state of development, how can one attribute the knowledge of a skilled teacher of this generation to one of the past, where perhaps half of his accumulated techniques, his personal innovation, were not present? And so today, trying to piece together a lineage of sorts in Escrima is a task needing a team of forensic specialists to determine what is "traditional" to the Philippines and what is "borrowed in" from other arts.

In my own research, I have looked to the past generation of masters to try to better understand these dynamic fighting arts. During the time of fabled masters such as the Saavedra and Romo clans of Cebu, Antonio Ilustrisimo, Benjamin Luna Lema, Anciong Bacon and others, there was no YouTube, no Internet, and no DVDs. But there was great distrust amongst those outside one's group, and thus very little cross-training. The arts were held close to the chest, imparted only to family members and students. The arts of this time period, for me, represent a treasure of what the original Filipino arts may have been like. This book, ***The Secret Art of Derobio Escrima***, offers us just such a glimpse into the art and life of an Escrima master of the past generation. The art of Braulio Pedoy.

This book presents in grand detail the often fantastical life and learning of Braulio Pedoy. From the small towns and jungles of the Philippines we learn how Pedoy came to meet his masters, perfect his skills and later bring the art to Hawaii. That Pedoy came to Hawaii like many Filipinos of his generation is nothing special. But the fact that he became one of the fabled escrimadors of that era in Hawaii, is especially noteworthy. He stood out amongst the likes of Floro Villabrille, Raymond Tobosa, Telesporo Subingsubing, Daniel Sisnores, and others whose arts and names became legendary even though few carry on their traditions today. Pedoy was the first to open an "open-door" club in Hawaii and saw to it that his art of Derobio would continue on. Grandmaster Dan Medina, one of Pedoy's disciples, has taken the mantle to ensure the art's continuation.

And so within the pages of this book are found the history, spiritual traditions, respects, basic strikes, systems of counters, locks and counter-locks of Derobio Escrima—an art preserved and  passed along intact from generation to generation, drawing a clear lineage of past teachers and present masters.

—Dr. Mark V. Wiley
Publisher, Tambuli Media

TABLE OF CONTENTS

CHAPTER 1

HISTORY OF DEROBIO ESCRIMA

Documented photo of General Faustino Ablin after his capture by 2nd Lt. Ralph A Jones, in command of a detachment of the eighth infantry and Philippine Scouts.

*Photo courtesy of J.F. Ptak

General Faustino Ablin

General Faustino Ablin was born on February 4th, 1854 on the Philippine island of Leyte, in the city of Ormoc. He was eighth out of nine children. According to various sources, he was not a very educated man yet he was a leader of many men. At first he was the leader of the Dios Dios Religious movement during the Spanish occupation of the Philippines. This was during a time when the poor of the Philippines were being taken advantage of by the upper castes, Spanish and Mestizos. What Ablin lacked for in education he more than made up for in motivation, character, and faith. How else could he command more than 500 men?

Faustino Ablin was more than just a mere bandit; he was also known as a patriot and a hero, depending on which side one was on. *Overland Monthly* and *Out West Magazine* (vol. 57) ran an article titled, "Justice Un-tempered," and quotes Governor Pedro Soler as saying that he considered Faustino Ablin "the greatest of the outlaw chiefs, with a huge army at his command."

General Ablin's constant harassment of the Spanish finally led to his capture and imprisonment sometime around the 1887-89 timeframe. The General was sent to a Spanish penal colony in Zamboanga, which is in the southernmost part of the Philippines. There he was kept imprisoned for the next 10 years.

It was said by Grandmaster Braulio Pedoy, that General Ablin led the forces of Leyte against the Spanish before the Spanish American War (1898). After the war Ablin was released from the penal colony, and made his way back to Leyte. Ablin refused to salute the American flag as long as it flew over the Philippine flag. He said, "Too many Filipino's died fighting for independence; besides we did not lose a war against the US so why should the American flag fly over it?" General Faustino Ablin saw no difference between the Spanish he had fought and been imprisoned by and the new American colonizers. He had fought for independence from

Spanish rulers. He now found himself confronted by the American government which, in Ablin's perspective, basically replaced the Spanish.

Ablin went from being the leader of the Dios Dios movement to taking the leadership of the Pulahan movement in Leyte. Faustino Ablin brought fear and apprehension to the Americans. He constantly harassed the new government and in doing so earned a huge price on his head. The Pulahan brought death and destruction with them and were reputed to be fearless. Before battle, the Pulahan went through religious rituals where they shaved their heads and tied whicker around their extremities. This served to slow their bleeding should they be injured or shot. This technique was remarkably effective. The Pulahan did not fear death; this movement was very strong in Leyte.

It was during this time period, that US soldiers found out that the military issue .38 caliber pistol and the Kraig rifle did little stop these religious foes. In response to this and what was also occurring in other parts of the Philippines, the US Government issued the .45 caliber pistol with its much needed stopping power. At least that's what the soldiers were told. They soon realized that even after being knocked down by the impact of the larger bullet, their determined foes often got up again only to decapitate their enemy. As a result, leather collars were issued to US soldiers in an effort to keep their heads from being cut off. Hence, the nickname "leather necks."

There are many stories about Faustino Ablin's capture and death. His death was exaggerated many times. Some say he was caught and hanged, others say he was taken away to never be heard from again. In the book *Policing America's Empire* by A.W. McCoy, Ablin's capture late in 1907 is mentioned; but again, it says nothing about his death.

GM Pedoy's account says he escaped and finally went deep into the Amandawin Mountains to live the life of a hermit. This falls in line with what is written in the "U.S. Congressional Serial Set" and the "Annual Report of the Secretary of War," printed by the U.S. government. This volume reports that 2nd Lt. Ralph A Jones, in command of a detachment of eight infantry and Philippine Scouts operating from La Paz, encountered Ablin in the Madagara River. Ablin was caught unawares, shot, and captured. In this official historical account General Faustino Ablin escaped six days after his capture. There is never any mention of his recapture to this day.

GGM Pedoy & Master Ron England

Grandmaster Braulio Tomada Pedoy

Master Pedoy served as body guard for Datu Piang, after defeating the previous body guard in bloody battle

*Photo courtesy of Siangco Family

I am honored to say that Grandmaster Braulio Pedoy was not only the most influential person in my martial arts career, but also something of a second father to me. His story is a tale almost mythical and folkloric in its own right. Close to the turn of the century, at a time of social unrest and brutality, when the many islands of the Philippines and their respective factions each fought for dominance over its neighbors, a young boy of about six years old embarked on a journey to escape the tyranny of a cruel and abusive father.

After receiving a particularly harsh beating one evening, the young Braulio decided it was time to leave all that he had known as home in the hope of a better life. Thin, alone, and with only a meager supply of provisions, he escaped his childhood residence and set off into the mountains without so much as a glance as to what he had left behind. It was a decision that would test his mind, body, and soul to the extreme.

The journey was a long one, and with what little he could afford to bring with him, starvation and dehydration proved a constant, grueling pair of combatants. After traveling just a short while, the young Pedoy was presented with his first obstacle: a fork in the road. One path was the familiar road to the city—where he knew he could surely find help and food—but this road ran the risk of him being found. In addition to this hindrance, he did not want to wind up with what he called the *piyo* (or rugged boys), a bunch of pick pockets and ruffians who made their living by stealing from others. The thought of becoming an immoral street rat was not one the boy found entirely appealing; especially when placed next to the second choice. This road lead deep into the mountainous jungles of the untamed Philippines. To Braulio, this path seemed the very embodiment of excitement and adventure. His choice was obvious. He chose the winding path through the mountains; quite literally a path that was destined to change his life forever.

Another painful lock applied on G.M. Medina

Grandmaster Pedoy and Grandmaster Subing

It was not long before what little food Braulio had brought were exhausted, and hunger set in once again. Even at his extraordinarily young age, the grandmaster-to-be demonstrated his level head and will to survive at any cost by observing what sort of foods the monkeys and boars ate. He reckoned that if the animals would eat it, it was safe for him as well. After four sleepless nights and five agonizingly draining days of travel, he happened upon a small shack nestled deep in the Amandiwin Mountains. At the time, nobody was there; only the smoke from a still-smoldering fire somebody had recently built. And so the young master waited until the occupant returned.

As it turns out, the owner was none other than General Faustino Ablin (*aka* Papa Ablen), who was more than shocked to come across a small boy sitting by his shack. He had thought no one would ever find him, much less a child. Years of exile and solitude certainly didn't prepare for this surprise. After questioning the boy and learning his tale, his surprise grew. How could such a child travel this great distance through the mountains and jungles which were laden with dangerous creatures, poisonous insects, wild animals and many unseen dangers. General Ablin asked the young boy if he had seen any snakes or any other deadly surprises along his journey, surprisingly, the answer was no. The general was a deeply religious man and considered this child to be sent by God. Ablin told Pedoy, "God has guided you to me." The next day Ablin told him, "I need to show you what's around here, so make sure you stay close to me or I will not be able to protect you." Off they went, and even though Braulio was young he had the hardest time keeping up with this 50+ year old who seemed to move like the wind. He was shown all the dangers that lurked in the mountains, including snakes that

Sr. Master Carlton Kramer with G.M. Pedoy

were big enough to fill a 55 gallon drum. General Ablin taught him the ways of the jungle as well as the art of Derobio Escrima.

G.M. Pedoy and G.M. Villabrille

For 11 years Pedoy learned and studied all his master had to teach him. Finally the day came when General Ablin announced that he had taught him all he had to teach and that it was time for Pedoy to go. "Tonight you will need to stand vigil and pray," Ablin said, and "make your peace with God, for tomorrow we fight." Braulio would have to face General Ablin for his final exam; a potentially-deadly one on one test of skills. Both men would be armed with bolos and it would be to the death. The reason that the exam was to the death was that there was no medical help within several days journey; if either of them would become seriously wounded, a slow miserable death would be eminent. Ablin told his young pupil, "If you are injured, I will kill you because I do not wish you to suffer and I expect you to do the same for me." With these ominous words ringing in his ears, Pedoy spent many sleepless hours awaiting his final test. At 17 Pedoy had the stamina youth could afford him, but it was equally matched by the experience of the now 62 year old general. Both used their best faints and counters. Braulio sustained three wounds; the first was across the bridge of his nose, the second at the base of his right thumb and the third under his chin. After almost three hours of intense fighting, both were exhausted. As hard as he had tried, Pedoy could not touch General Ablin; but he had survived the skirmish. These were scars that he proudly wore as badges of honor.

Sr. High Chief Knut Peacock and G.M. Pedoy

Next, Ablin took Braulio to a mountain pond. He told Braulio to climb to the top of the tree that looked over the pond. Ablin said, "Look down into the water and tell me what you see?" Braullio said he saw a bunch of bamboo stakes just below the surface of the water. "Now," the general said, "jump!" The young man was hesitant to do so. Again, General Ablin commanded him to do so, saying, "Have faith, jump!" And jump he did. Much to Pedoy's amazement, he didn't die. He wasn't even hurt when he hit the water, and when he looked around, he saw no bamboo stakes; he only saw bamboo leaves floating on the surface of the water. It was only an illusion the general had created to test the mental and spiritual skills he needed to survive. Braullio Pedoy was now ready to go out into the world but the general had a few more lessons to share.

"Study the movements of the trees and the ocean," he told his pupil, "for they both have lessons to teach. Observe the motion of the branches in the wind. The tree stands strong, yet the branches pass the power of the wind as you must pass a blow and return to an equal and balanced position before reaching out with your own counter." Next he said, "Climb to the top of the highest tree and look out unto the ocean." He told his young student, "You will see different shades of blue, the darker the blue the deeper the water. In the lighter areas it is shallow, rough and noisy. Many are at this level. Close minded people with conflicting goals in life tend to use their mouths loosely. We must strive for the deeper water where it's calm and peaceful, where your morals run deep and only pure thoughts come out of your mouth. Thus you can observe for yourself what is shallow and what is deep. Now it's time for you to leave. Go Island to Island and learn from all the different masters. When you're done, make your way to America where you will do well." The young Pedoy wished his master a good life and embarked on his next journey.

Datu Piang
*Photo courtesy of Piang.net

Before traveling to other islands, Pedoy decided to stop at his home to visit his father. But the visit was not well received. After seeing things had not changed much, Braulio continued onward. After traveling to many of the Islands and studying from as many masters as would teach him, Braulio found that every village had different styles of fighting. Pedoy once said that some systems relied on sound—once the crack of weapons was heard, that was the indicator to counter the attack. One of the last places the young Pedoy found himself was in the southern Philippines. There, he said that the Moro fighters had incorporated a special skill that was adapted to their environment. Living primarily on or near beaches, these fighters used footwork that sprayed their opponent's faces with sand as they fought, crippling their eyes with sharp blinding shrapnel. This technique was unique but also limited as they relied upon it heavily and found themselves somewhat handicapped on more solid ground. But on sand it was like fighting a whirlwind. This and many more things he learned.

Later in his travels the young master found himself in Mindanao, there he was presented with yet another challenge. Rumors of a fierce fighter, Datu Piang's bodyguard, who was terrorizing the town's people, reached his ears. Many told tales of rape, extortion and bullying. Although the young Braulio was new to this town he felt something had to be done. So he entered a tournament the bodyguard was fighting in. Much like in the old movies, many of the towns people turned up to watch justice hopefully be served. The battle lasted only a few minutes, each looking for an opening as they tested each other's defenses. As circle after circle was paced in the sand each combatant scanned the other for weaknesses. Pedoy's sharp eye found a slight moment of distraction, and took his chance. It was just enough for him to inflict a critical blow, shattering the man's left collar bone. The spectators cheered and, caught up in their own quest for vengeance, chanted a request for death. "Kill him! Kill him!" they chanted and yelled "kill him!" Master Pedoy heard the words of his master ringing clear in his mind, of showing mercy to those who could not defend themselves. He looked at the angry crowd and said, "You want to kill him?" He threw his weapon on the ground. "You want him dead? You do it!" He turned his back and walked away leaving the injured man to tend to his wounds and perhaps learn a lesson from this encounter. Having

G.G.M. Pedoy demonstrating the use of double bolos

defeated and disabled Datu Piang's bodyguard, Pedoy was now offered the vacant position. His salary was 100 pesos a month. Pedoy then traveled far and wide, his travels reaching as far as Borneo where he studied the movements of the Dayak head hunters. Master Pedoy loved to tell tales of his travels.

The Brilliante Tribe

While following his master's instructions of traveling from island to island to learn as much as he could from as many masters as possible, Pedoy found himself in a very mountainous region on a narrow muddy path, a result of the recent rains. This made for a treacherous journey, with the mountain rising up on one side and a steep down slope on the other. Along with it being an extremely remote location, the last thing the young Pedoy thought would happen did. With one

misplaced step, he lost his footing and slipped, hurtling down the side of the jungle covered mountain. When he finally came to a stop, he painfully realized in addition to many cuts and scrapes his shoulder was dislocated. Knowing that there wouldn't be anyone coming along to help him, Pedoy knew that it was up to him to reposition his shoulder. After a while, he finally saw what he was looking for; a tree with exposed roots on the side of the mountain. He managed to squeeze his hand though a small hole in the roots. After a few ginger test pulls, he balled his hand into a fist and hurtled himself back in a single brutal motion. A yelp escaped his lips, as his shoulder was sent back into its original place. The excruciating pain flushed over his body and the soothing black of unconsciousness took over. When he awoke

GGM & Ron 1988

he found himself in what seemed to be an enormous cavern. He was not alone. He was being cared for by what appeared to be a primitive tribe and although that in itself would not have been unusual, the fact that they were fair skinned was. This tribe referred to themselves as the Brilliante people. An isolated group that had little to no contact with the other tribes in the area. He also learned that they possessed some remarkable abilities that included the arts of moving through the jungles unseen and unheard a well, as skillful navigation of the endless caverns that were in the area. This amazing tribe cared for Master Pedoy's injuries and nursed him back to health. Once he had recovered, Pedoy was given some food and sent on his way. The only payment they accept for their services was a promise from Braulio to keep their home a secret.

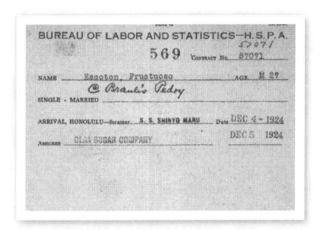

From the Docks of Manila to Hawaii

Eventually the young Master Pedoy found himself working on the docks of Manila as a longshore man. But he knew that was not the life for him. He could still hear his master's words ringing in his ears, "Travel to America." So, around 1924, he took his chance and, using his friend's workman's papers, he booked passage on the steamer S.S. Shinyo Maru, under the assumed name of Escoton Fructouso, and made his way to Hawaii, arriving there on December 4th, 1924. On December 5th, he was quickly assigned work on the Ola'a sugar cane plantation. All the workers were bundled to work together. The Chinese were grouped with other Chinese and the Filipinos were grouped with other Filipinos. This was a good time for Filipino martial arts because it gave the different practitioners a chance to train together. The inner secrets, however, were not shared with others.

Grandmaster Pedoy and the Supernatural

Although a very religious man, Braulio Pedoy had many strong convictions and beliefs that delved into the realm of the supernatural. As in many old countries, there is often a subtle blend between religion, folklore and superstition. Having spent most of his impressionable years in the Philippine jungles, Pedoy adapted many of the local beliefs which were mixed with Christianity. One of his favorite tales included the belief in the *anting-anting*, using the magical power of words, charms and prayers. The charms could be anything from small amulets, human knee caps or bones, to vials of holy oils. I remember that he wore a belt under his cloths that contained some of these items. One night I asked if he would show it to me and to my surprise he did. The belt was made of cloth with sealed pockets. Inside, he claimed to have various small bones, some of them human knee caps. He offered out the pouch containing one of the knee caps. "Try to touch this, and watch how it runs away from you," he said with an impish grin on his face. As hard as I tried it kept slipping from my grasp. I spent many a night listening to his many tales.

Kavai Park Luau honoring Kali Grandmaster Floro Villabrille (seated). Front row: G.M. Braulio Pedoy, Zena Sixtana Babao and Joey Del Mar. Back row: Richard Bustillo, Ben Largusa, Lucky Lucay -lucay and Dan Inosanto.

One tale was about the heart of the banana tree. In the Philippines banana trees grew everywhere. This story started in the cemetery as yet another challenge in his life. Pedoy spent many a night in the cemetery where he would go at night and wait for the banana tree flower to bloom. As the legend goes, if you can catch the seed of the flower when it blooms, it will give you special powers. This kind of reminds me of the plains Indians and peyote they use in their spiritual ceremonies. But before these powers can be bestowed the receiver must prove his worthiness by battling spirits. Whether the seed caused hallucinations or actual apparitions came, we will never know. But master Pedoy tells of a great battle between himself and these unearthly attackers. Even a short glance into these spirits eyes could leave you mesmerized and defenseless, which would result in your death. Pedoy reveals the key to survival was not to gaze at the eyes but focus on the chest instead. Master Pedoy survived this ordeal and was awarded the special powers he was seeking, his rarely seen ability to control the bleeding of

Peter Schmall, Knut Peacock, Ron England, Dan Medina, Master Pedoy

wounds as well as his bodily functions. He has been known to pierce his tongue, hand and forearms using a piece of bamboo with no visible signs of blood.

While writing this story, another tale came to mind. In his youth Pedoy had said that when most Filipinos arrived in Hawaii they were expected to work in the cane and pineapple fields, but doing hard labor and working like a mule was not for him. Luckily Grandmaster Pedoy was a very good gambler and was able to make a living at it. Also we must remember the time period was the great depression and Hawaii was a very hard place. On the plantations the workers were worked dawn to dusk and to the point of exhaustion for very little pay. As usual, Pedoy would wait untill the workers got paid and he would gamble with them, winning most of the time. One night, though, he gambled with a sore loser who was livid at having lost his pay. Then late one night the sore looser spent several hours waiting in the shadows, plotting his revenge. He got ready to ambush the young gambler as he passed by. As Pedoy passed the dark alley, he was unexpectedly attacked by the disgruntled loser who jumped out

Cas Magda, Martinez, Master Pedoy, Dan Inosanto,
Richard Bustillo, Peter Schmall

from his hiding place and buried his dagger deep into the master's belly. A few seconds later, the attacker was battered, bruised and unconscious with master Pedoy sitting on him while waiting for the police and ambulance to arrive. Master Pedoy was rushed to the hospital, but on arrival he was pronounced DOA (dead on arrival). The truth was, he had actually slowed down his heart beat and breathing so he would not bleed out. At the hospital he was tagged and left in the emergency room, covered with only a thin white sheet in preparation for transfer to the morgue on the next shift.

That night as one of the nurses was making her rounds, Master Pedoy awoke and upon seeing the nurse, sat up and yelled out, "Excuse me, but I'm freezing! Get me a blanket!" The poor startled nurse ran out of the room screaming.

Magical Tree in a Bottle

The next item the grandmaster showed me was a small bottle of oil that was always in his pocket. This is what he used when doing hilot, a type of healing massage which resembles acupressure but with holy words being spoken as it is being done. It is said that Pedoy cured a pinched nerve that Guru Dan Inosanto had, that no other doctor could resolve. This oil was also used in exorcism and all manners of healing. People came from all over seeking Pedoy's help. He never asked for money; if you were able to make a donation he would accept that. These donations would accumulate and when he could he would travel to the Philippines. The money would always go to the church of the famous healing shrine of the Potenciana, also known as the Saranza Chapel on the Island of Bohol. This was the home of Mrs. Pedoy and her relatives, so they tried to make a yearly visit. On one of these visits in a gesture of thanks the caretaker of the chapel gave Grandmaster Pedoy a bottle of wax from all the spent candles burning on the chapels alter. He gratefully thanked the old caretaker and when he arrived home he placed the bottle on his home alter. A few years later Pedoy had a stroke that paralyzed one side of his body. One evening while in bed Pedoy glanced towards his alter and he remembered the bottle from the healing shrine and asked his wife to bring it to him. To his great astonishment the wax had melted into oil and there was a very small tree growing inside. He wondered how a tree could grow in wax oil. It must be a sign, he thought. He then started to massage himself with this oil and pray and soon found himself feeling better. In a couple of weeks, he was cured! In order to always keep the bottle full, he replaced what oil was used with coconut oil. As time passed the tree continued to grow, along with the legend of it's and master Pedoy's healing powers. Many a famous Escrimador visited and asked that he share this oil with them, to no avail. This was only shared with his inner circle of students that had achieved full instructor status and only one outsider that I'm aware of—the Babao Family. As for the healing massage, that was taught to Chief Peter Schmall and Carlton Kramer, who were taught so they would be able to massage the grandmaster. As to the prayer or *oracion* of Pedoy, that was shared with only family members and the red shirt instructors of the original Pedoy's school of Derobio Escrima.

Pearl Harbor, December 7th 1941

Grandmaster Pedoy had a very interesting life filled with many adventures. He was present during the bombing of Pearl Harbor on that frightful day that Japan attacked the U.S. During this now infamous time period, Pedoy was employed at the Schollfield Barracks as a security guard and also started training U.S. service men in hand to hand combat. One day, a student who had been deployed returned to the base, and upon seeing Master Pedoy, he dropped to his knees and kissed the master's feet. The emotional soldier explained through tears if it had not been for the training he received from Master Pedoy, he would not be here today. He went on to tell the harrowing tale of battle in which his platoon found themselves in direct confrontation with a Japanese platoon. After a long firefight, both sides ran out of ammunition and the command was given to "fix Bayonets." The soldier, however, did as Master Pedoy had taught him. He took his bayonet and employed it like a bolo knife. The engagement with the Japanese was fierce and soldiers on both sides were dropping quickly. All he could remember was passing the blows and countering, cutting, slashing, stabbing and constantly moving to the outside of his enemies as he had done in training many times. It soon all became a blur and when it was all over, he was the only one left standing.

Later in life, Pedoy worked for Gas Pro Inc. In 1961 Pedoy opened the first Escrima school on the Hawaiian Islands that was open to all races. This was a time when martial arts were not shared with people not of Asian descent. On April 9th, 1976, the state of Hawaii and the House of Representatives passed house resolution number 633, honoring him as an Escrima expert extraordinaire. In 1991 Grandmaster Pedoy was inducted into the International Martial Arts Hall of Fame for his outstanding contributions to the Philippine Martial art of Escrima. All of the Hawaii schools of Kali, Arnis and Escrima were in attendance to honor this legendary man. Also in attendance were Grandmaster Richard Bustillo and, representing Guro Dan Innosanto, Burton Richardson, who also presented Master Pedoy with awards of accomplishment and gratitude.

Pedoy Hall of Fame

Grandmaster Dan Medina

Grandmaster Dan Medina

Photo Credit: Steve R. Leimberg

I was born in Brooklyn, New York in 1953. At the age of 17, I enlisted in the U.S. Navy and spent the next 22 years circling the globe two-and-a-half times. My first real martial arts training started in Puerto Rico around 1973. The U.S. Navy introduced me to a combination of Judo and the Navy Seal Quick-Kill method as part of my training. This was not only the spark that ignited the flame but the beginning to an intensive martial arts career.

In 1977, I was assigned to the USS Hitchiti, an ocean going tug. It was during this assignment that I was introduced to the Black Masters Sphinx Karate Clan of the Philippines by Master Ricardo Mendoza.

It is a very eclectic style of martial arts that looks like a combination of Karate, Kung-fu and Filipino martial arts. However, getting into this class was not so easy, you could not just walk in and say you wanted to train. I was first put through a test. These days, most students would probably walk away from such a trial. The sun was at about a 45-degree angle and I was put into what my teacher called a sumo stance, sort of like a horse stance. I was told to watch the sun go down and of course after a few minutes my legs started to tremble. I started to get up and was told to get back down or it would hurt even more. I tried to stay there, but now the pain was really intense. I attempted to get up again. This time I was told if I got up I might as well go home and that I would not be able to be part of the class. So I stayed and by now my whole body was trembling and the pain could clearly be seen in my face. The sweat was pouring and I could not hold the tears back. After the sun went down I was told that was it for the day's training. The next morning when I woke up I jumped out of bed like I always did, but this time I did not land on my feet—I did a full body slam down onto the floor. My legs could not bear the weight. Every muscle hurt and it took all I had to stand up, my legs and thighs hurt so bad that I actually had to pivot my hips to walk. That night, to everyone's surprise, I showed up to class. The rest is history.

Dan 1980s

After about eight months of intensive training, Master Mendoza took us to Baguio which is in the northern mountainous part of the Philippines. The local Sphinx group prepared a grueling training session that lasted several days. Starting from 5:00 am until 10:00 pm, the training was intense and the Masters expected 110%. We were taught breathing exercises while at the same time conditioning our finger tips on the concrete gym floor. We also conditioned our bodies to take punishment. While we performed our breathing the teachers would go by and either punch us or kick us while we exhaled and if you did not do the breathing right you would end up doubled over on the floor. It was also here that I was introduced to Arnis 63 Generals—the art that started me on my road to FMA. On our last day, a martial arts tournament was staged just for us. We were expected to fight and use our new skills. Thanks to the excellent instructors, we fought and none of us ended up with any serious injuries. It was an experience I will never forget!

In 1978, I was reassigned to the City of Olongapo in the Philippines. Sphinx Karate did not have a presence in this part of the Philippines so I joined P.M.A.S. (Philippine Martial Arts Studio) where I studied Kyokushin and Kuntaw under Master Reynaldo Ginco.

I still remember the pain those hands of steel could inflict. Ginco was known for his ability to crush bed rock stones with his bare hands! It was also something I got to feel. One day while sparing I had thrown a front kick and he showed me why the training was so hard on conditioning of the hands and feet. All he did was throw a back fist combined with an open hand block on my shin, it was a direct attack to my attack. For the next few weeks I limped, and to this day I believe he gave me a small hairline fracture of my right shin bone. From then on I was conditioning my hands on the makiwara (Okinawan striking post).

Front Row, left to right: GM Medina, Unknown. Back Row, left to right: Batikan Edwardo Pedoy, Mrs. Pedoy and GGM Braulio Pedoy

Around 1981 Master Gingco took us to compete at the Karate Tournament at Clarke Air Force Base. These tournaments were pretty rough; no pads or protection of any kind, it was bare knuckle. That day in the Philippines is one I won't forget as I had my ribs fractured and the guy that did that to me had his ankle broken by a sipa kick immediately after. I was out of commission for about two months. The funny thing was that I did not feel the pain right away. It was after I got back home to Subic and took a nap and had time for the adrenalin to wear off, that when I tried to get out of bed that the pain hit me! Lucky I was young and healed in two months.

In the Philippines, I had the opportunity to put my skills to use and define what was practical and what

GM Dan Medina and wife Stephanie with Soke Michael Kinney

Professor Al De la Cruz, GM Dan Medina, High Chief Antionette Chavez, unknown and GM Richard Bustillio at Medina's yearly Martial Arts Camp

One of the New Mexico Derobio Escrima branches; Maestro Adam Wolf, Chief Maestra Antionette Chavez, GGM Dan Medina, Maestro Gene Wolf and Maestro Gathan Garcia.

wasn't in "real time" street situations. On loan to the Provost Marshall during a time of Martial Law, I was required to enforce the law without the aid of a firearm. This was a really dangerous time and we really got to learn the sleeper hold well. We used to keep tally as to who choked out the most people in one night, but that was not my preferred method at all. I would only use a sleeper as a last resort. We even had a saying in the AFP (Armed Forces Police), "When in doubt, choke them out." In fact, we actually had tee-shirts made with that saying on them, but we were soon told we could not wear them anymore; they were not politically correct, after all.

I really felt at this time that martial arts had to be practical and no-nonsense so I continued my search for more training. In addition to practicing Arnis 63 Generals, exchanging techniques with my roommate who was taking Aikido, I also continued my tutelage with Master Gingco whenever possible. You could say I was breathing, eating, and sleeping martial arts. I just couldn't get enough.

Around 1980, I found myself stationed on the USS Belleauwood LHA-3, a marine amphibious carrier. This is where I first met Dan Inosanto while the ship was in dry dock. We hit it off instantly and I got an autographed book from him titled, *The Filipino Martial Arts*. To this day we are still friends. The ship finally got underway and was heading toward San Diego when one day I spotted someone on the flight deck that looked strangely familiar.

After confirming my suspicions by checking the by now well-read book about the Filipino Martial arts, I could hardly believe my luck! Master Narrie Babao, the first full contact stick fighting champion of the U.S. was on my ship! I mustered up the courage to approach him and introduced myself which was instantly followed by asking Master Babao if I could become a student. My expectations were crushed however when Master Babao graciously refused and informed me he wasn't accepting any new students at this time. I wasn't one for giving up so a few days later, when I found out Master Babao was in quarantine with the chicken pox, I knew it was my opportunity to change his mind. Chicken pox is not something most Filipinos are exposed to as children and it can be quite severe when you catch it as an adult. Master Babao's Filipino friends wanted nothing to do with catching the chicken pox so they stayed as far away as you possibly could on a ship. I already had the chicken pox as a child, so I quickly became Master Babao's only link to the "outside." I brought him martial arts magazines, shared news and goings on from the ship, and generally just kept him company.

Dan Medina, Lee Davis and Melcor Chavez gearing up for sparing.

When the ship pulled into port, Master Babao was still in quarantine, so he threw his car keys at me and asked me to take his car to his wife, Zena. "While you're there," he said. "Tell her that you're my new student." I couldn't believe my ears! I don't remember the drive to Master's house but I do remember his wife, Zena, telling me how lucky I was and that it was a rare thing indeed for her husband to accept new students. He had turned many away over the years and she was almost as surprised as I was at the news.

For the next four years I trained diligently under the watchful eyes of Master Babao. To say he was a perfectionist would be an understatement. As a student of Master Babao, you repeat a technique over and over and over again until it is perfected before you're allowed to move to the next. I remember one time, when I was a black shirt under Master Babao, he sent me and his young son, Jack, to Singleton's Karate Tournament under the guidance of his wife, Zena. That day I took 2nd place in forms and Jack Babao took first place in the Black Belt Weapons divisions. This was also the first time I fought in the full contact weapons division, which proved to be quite interesting. Right at the get-go, I

Chief Maestro Mike Wanke, Maestra Amalie Frischknecht, Assistant Maestra Stephanie Medina and GGM Dan Medina

GM Dan Medina with Chief Maestro Arlan Sanford (Co-founder of Dog Brothers)

GM Medina with top ranking High Chief Maestro Brandon Jordan

destroyed my opponent's shinai (split bamboo training sword).

I stopped, not wanting to hit a defenseless man. My opponent got another weapon and again I destroyed it in the first few seconds. This continued for several rounds. I probably could have won that fight but keeping my honor and not hitting an unarmed man was more important to me. My second fight that day, was against a skilled nunchaku fighter. It was over before it started as the nunchaku flew off into the crowd and I was again left with an unarmed opponent. I was awarded with third place since I never "finished" the fights. After the tournament was over, I was instantly surrounded by spectators and other martial artists curious about the type of martial arts I practiced. I simply replied, "It's Arnis-Kuntao/Batangas Narrie Babao's family style. They all agreed, if the fights had been "real-life" situations, the winner would have been the one still holding his weapon.

As I traveled with the Navy, I continued to study with Master Narrie Babao and Master Ricardo Mendoza. At every port, I looked for classes and instructors to continue my education and broaden my experience. From Hong Kong, Japan, Korea, Thailand, Singapore, to Sri Lanka and, of course, the Philippines, I sought out anyone who could give me more to learn, more to experience and more technique!

In 1984, I was assigned to the Sea Bees (PhibCB1) as a small arms and combat instructor. It was during this time that I met Philip Pabalinas who, in exchange for being taught Kuntao, taught me the Ocho system and Modern Arnis, Ernesto Presas style.

Later, in 1986, I found out that my next assignment would take me to Hawaii. Narrie Babao instructed me to do two things when I arrived there. The first was to seek out as an instructor Snookie Sanches, a famous escrimador who had studied with Grandmaster Floro Villabrille, a full-contact champion of the Philippines. The second was to visit and offer his and my respects to the Grandmaster Braulio Pedoy, who was retired and no longer teaching. My plane landed, I checked into my hotel and per my instructions, I wasted no time in calling GM Pedoy. To my surprise, I was invited to come see him that very night. I'll never forget meeting Braulio T. Pedoy for the first time. He was already 89 years old and he was small in size. His heavily wrinkled face had a quick smile and steely eyes. His son, Eduardo J. Pedoy, was also there and the three of us had a great time talking about the martial arts and how much I wanted to learn Escrima. I'm not sure exactly what I did to impress him but that night, he told me that if I really wanted to learn Escrima, that he would teach me.

For the next few years, I absorbed everything I could about the secrets of Derobio Escrima. One night Batikan Eduardo Pedoy, who was then the Chief Instructor, surprised me by saying, "You don't know how lucky you are! You're getting stuff I wasn't even taught!" Batikan Eduardo Pedoy often worked late in the evenings and missed many of his father's classes.

Batikan Pedoy & Maestro Lee Davis

GM Pedoy also realized this and felt the need to pass on his 144 counters or they would be lost forever. With his new mission in focus we started on an intensive regimen of training that not only included the techniques but also the history of the Filipino martial arts. This time period was taxing, physically (my wrists hurt for weeks), mentally, and even spiritually.

Hawaii in the 1980s was a variable Mecca of martial arts. I was like a kid in a candy store and it didn't take me long to develop strong friendships with the leaders and founders of the most prominent art forms. Bobby Lowe, James Miyaji, Pat Nakata, Ken Funakoshi, Tomu Arakawa, Sung Au and Joe Bunch were just a few of the great people I came to know and admire.

I was both surprised and honored when Joe Bunch, then president of the Hawaii Karate Congress, sponsored me as an instructor. After a secretive, closed door voting process, I was accepted into the organization. For me, this was an incredible honor since many hopeful instructors, some I knew and called friends, were turned away. To this day, I attribute a lot of my knowledge about general martial arts history and culture to these gentlemen and will forever be grateful to them.

Top Escrimador Masters: left to right: Bram Franks, Gerome Barber, Jimmy Tacosa, Dan Medina, Raffy Pambuan and Abundio Baet

Joe Bunch was an old time instructor who trained with some of the founding fathers of Karate. Sensei Tatsuo Shimabaku, the founder of Isshin-ryu Karate, and Sensei Seikichi Odo, of the Okinawa Karate Kobudo Federation. Master Bunch decided to take me under his wing and share his knowledge with me at night, and so we would train at the Arizona Memorial away from all eyes. I wish I could remember more, but it's so much. I think that I have forgotten more than most people know.

During this amazing time, I skippered a small ocean going Navy vessel that traveled between Honolulu and Kauai. This was where I met Greg Lontayao and had the opportunity to visit the original Kali grandmaster, Floro Villabrille, in Kapaa. He showed me the certificate that was issued by the then Governor General Murphy proclaiming Villabrille the champion of the Philippines in stick-fighting. As if that wasn't incredible in itself, before leaving his house he had me kneel down and face the sun. He placed his hand on my head and proceeded to place a blessing on me. I had only been blessed like this once before (by GM Pedoy upon being promoted to full instructor in Derobio Escrima). This memory will stay with me always.

Ron England demonstrating knife defense

My next military assignment took me to Albuquerque, New Mexico. I contacted a local school with hopes of being able to teach. As luck would have it, I got a hold of Shihan Ray Barerra, who was the first non-Japanese to win the All Japan Karate Championship in kata. He is also an International Karate and Kickboxing & International Martial Arts Hall of Fame instructor. Barerra asked me to show him what I did and after giving him a brief demonstration of my skills, he marched into his office and began calling all the other Martial Arts schools in Albuquerque. This part of the country had never been exposed to my type of Philippine martial arts and I was treated like the new "hot commodity." I received offers from many schools to teach and from many others to do seminars. I had spent years accumulating knowledge and I was ready to share it with anyone who wanted to learn.

Founders of General Ablin School of Escrima: Chief Master Gary Largo, Chief Master Leslie Largo, Senior Master Carlton Cramer, Senior High Chief Knut Peacock and Senior High Chief Peter Schmall

As a result of this firestorm, today there are close to 1,000 Escrima students in the

Tuhon Chaz Siangco

Pulahan Derobio Escrima founders Chaz Siangco, Christian P. Siangco & Christopher P. Singco

Albuquerque / Santa Fe area. Of the students I am proud to have taught, some of the more famous ones are Arlan "Salty Dog" Sanford, my protégé Prof. Brandon Jordan (who is now teaching in the Miami area), Chief Instructor Antionette Chavez (Owner of Takai Mine Karate, who continues to represent Majapai in New Mexico), and Chief Instructor Melcor Chavez. Then there are those that made instructor and will only teach privately and not in a commercial setting, including Chief instructors Gene and Adam Wolf, Gathan Garcia, Mike Wanke and Amalie Fritshnecht, to name a few.

Many skilled and well-known instructors call New Mexico their home. This offered me the opportunity to train in Serrada Escrima with Bruce Albach, and exchange ideas with Master Jimmy Tacosa and one of the most famous MMA instructors in the USA today, Greg Jackson.

At one time, during a summer camp in New Mexico, I demonstrated how to defend against multiple opponents. Seated among the audience was Richard Bustillo. After my performance, he told me, "I know Derobio, and what you did was create a new animal." To me that was a great compliment, coming from the mouth of one of Bruce Lee's training partners.

Currently, I am the founder and grandmaster of what I call Majapai, the culmination of my martial art training and experiences. I am Regional High Chief in Derobio Escrima under GGM Braulio Pedoy, and Rajah (6th degree red & white belt) and Florida Vice-President for Sphinx Karate & Arnis 63 Generals under Ricardo Mendoza and the Father of Sphinx Karate, Jimmy B. Galez. I also hold a 3rd dan in Kobudo under Shihan Ray Barrera and have received an honorary Doctorate for my contributions to the martial arts from the Euro Technical University. Grandmaster Sam Allred also awarded me an honorary Black Belt for my contributions to the art of Kajukenbo.

Medina and Jordan with GGM Pedoy photo

After 9/11, I donated my services to pilots and flight attendants, teaching them bladed weapons defense techniques. In August of 2001, I was inducted into the International Karate and Kickboxing Hall of Fame by Dan Sword, and Shihan Ray Barrera made the presentation of the plaque.

In November of 2009, I was inducted into the Eastern USA International-al Blackbelt Hall of Fame for "my outstanding contributions to the martial arts" by Shihan John Kovacs. In January of 2010, I had the honor of being inducted into the Action Martial Arts Magazine Hall of Honors, and later that year named Escrima Instructor of the Year by the World Head of Family Sokeship Council. In March 2011, I was inducted as the newest member of the World Head of Family Sokeship Council which was a great honor for me. In 2013, I was presented with the Silver Lifetime Achievement Award (for over 39 years of teaching Martial Arts) and in the spring of 2014, I was awarded as a Legendary Grandmaster of the Martial Arts by WHFSC.

In my martial arts journey, I have truly been blessed by the many individuals I had the honor of studying with, befriending and teaching. I currently reside with my wife, Stephanie, and youngest son Michael, in Kingsland, Georgia. My son Donald, lives in Phoenix, Arizona;

my son Melvin, lives in Albuquerque, New Mexico; and my son Steven, lives in Tampa, Florida. After having taught at several schools in the area, a few years ago I opened my own school in Fernandina Beach on Amelia Island (near the Florida/Georgia border) and hold classes in St. Mary's, Georgia as well. My seminar schedule keeps me traveling quite a bit, always offering me the opportunity to see old friends.

For more information please visit my website: majapai.com

Dan with Kris

Dan and Corwin Drakus

Dan with Kris

Dan and Lee

International Karate and Kickboxing hall of fame

Derobio Family Lineage

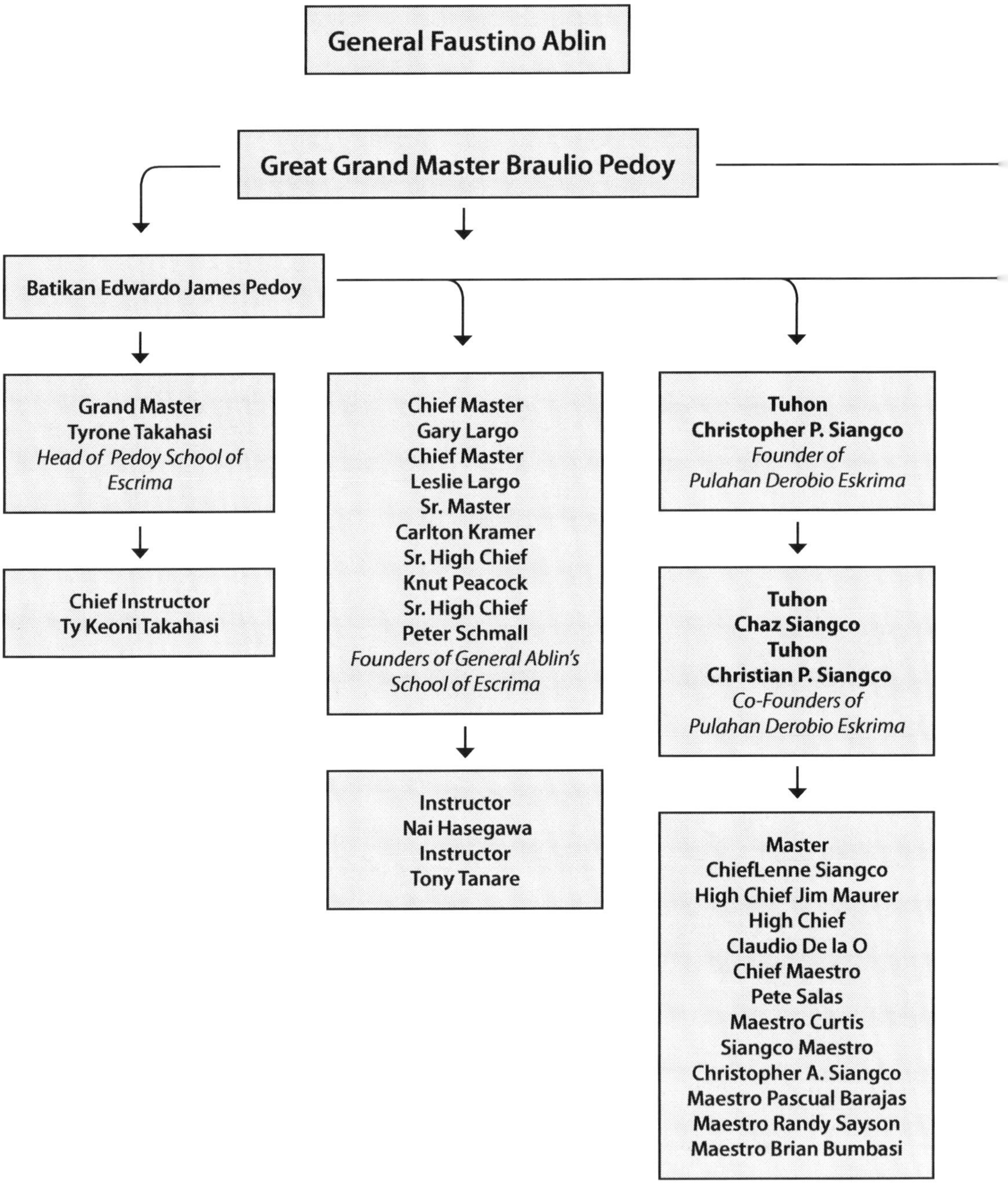

General Faustino Ablin

Great Grand Master Braulio Pedoy

Batikan Edwardo James Pedoy

**Grand Master
Tyrone Takahasi**
*Head of Pedoy School of
Escrima*

**Chief Instructor
Ty Keoni Takahasi**

**Chief Master
Gary Largo
Chief Master
Leslie Largo
Sr. Master
Carlton Kramer
Sr. High Chief
Knut Peacock
Sr. High Chief
Peter Schmall**
*Founders of General Ablin's
School of Escrima*

**Instructor
Nai Hasegawa
Instructor
Tony Tanare**

**Tuhon
Christopher P. Siangco**
*Founder of
Pulahan Derobio Eskrima*

**Tuhon
Chaz Siangco
Tuhon
Christian P. Siangco**
*Co-Founders of
Pulahan Derobio Eskrima*

**Master
ChiefLenne Siangco
High Chief Jim Maurer
High Chief
Claudio De la O
Chief Maestro
Pete Salas
Maestro Curtis
Siangco Maestro
Christopher A. Siangco
Maestro Pascual Barajas
Maestro Randy Sayson
Maestro Brian Bumbasi**

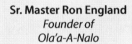

Sr. Master Ron England *Founder of* *Ola'a-A-Nalo*	**Grand Master Dan Medina** *Founder of* *Majapai Derobio*

Sr. Chief Instructor Thomas Whippy Sr. Chief Instructor Bert Mier Chief Instructor Patrick Rudder Chief Instructor Daniel Breazeal Chief Instructor Randy Cabanilla Chief Instructor Dexter James Sr. Maestro Gary Schroder Maestro Frank Krau Maestro Joe Tibay Maestro Steve de Castillo	High Chief Brandon Jordan High Chief Melcor Chavez High Chief Antionette Chavez Sr. Chief Maestro Lee Davis Chief Maestro Arlan Sanford Chief Maestro Mike Wanke Chief Maestra Margarita Chavez Chief Maestra Angelica Chavez Maestro Joey Chavez Maestro Gene Wolfe Maestro Adam Wolfe Maestra Amalie Frischknecht Maestro Marty Aragon Maestro Gathan Garcia Maestra Peggy Chavez Maestro Edwin Telles Maestro T.J. Trujillo Maestra Judy Prieto Maestro Henry Gamboa Maestro Blain Warrior

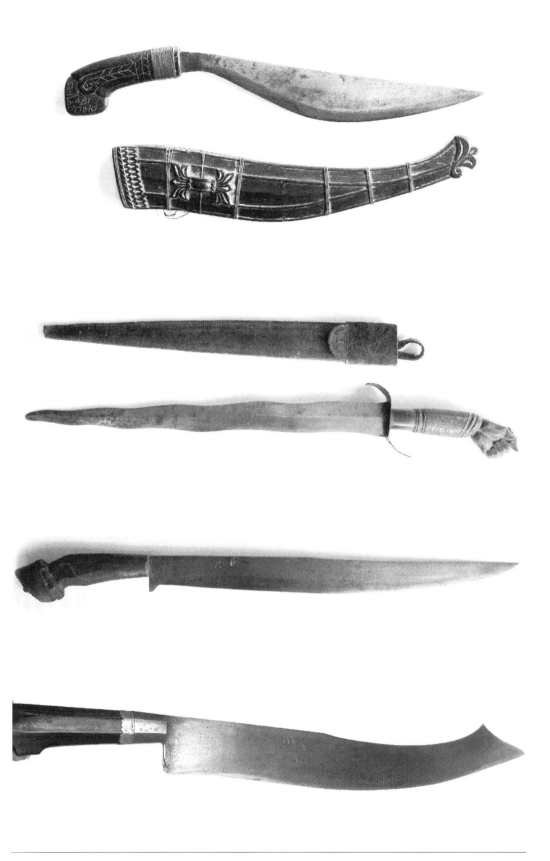

CHAPTER 2

WEAPONS OF DEROBIO ESCRIMA

Like many Filipino martial arts, Grandmaster Braulio Pedoy's Derobio Escrima system is composed of techniques that can universally be applied to the empty hands and almost any weapon. In fact, Pedoy often told us it didn't matter which weapon we used as long as we had an understanding of the specific use of both sticks and bolos. However, the three main weapons used within the system are described below.

Garote—The garote or "Escrima stick" can be made of fire-hardened rattan vines. These are good for training because they are flexible and can absorb shock. Kamagong (Philippine iron wood) and bahi (the center of the Philippine palm), are for used for fighting and will definitely crush bone.

Bolo—The bolo is a machete-type weapon; it can be short or long, light or heavy. Its characteristics of length and weight will dictate the type of movements that can be used with it—fast and small movements or large and heavy blows. The bolo saw much use not only as a weapon, but also as a farm and jungle tool. In the Philippines, the bolo is used to cut sugar cane and for cutting paths through the mountainous jungles of Leyte.

Talibon—The talibon is reminiscent of the Nepalese national weapon, the kukri knife. The talibon has a heavy curve that swings up to a sharp point. This weapon is used in slicing and chopping motions capable of severing limbs, in addition to its thrusting capabilities. The talibon's cutting ability lead to it being the favored weapon of the Philippine insurgent group, the Pulahan.

Other Weapons of the Philippines

The Philippines is a vast island chain with nearly 100 ethno-linguistic groups and cultures. There are hundreds of fighting styles and weapons to go with them. In addition to the three main weapons used in Derobio Escrima, some of the other well-known weapons of Filipino martial arts are described below.

Kris—The kris of the Philippines is different from that of Indonesia in that it is bigger and heavier, thus requiring larger movements. The Philippine kris can have numerous curves, a straight blade, or a combination of both. Its double edge gives it the ability to cut with forward and rear cutting motions, in addition to thrusting. These weapons are well made, with pattern wielded steel blade construction or even Damascus (watered steel construction). During the Filipino-American War a faster, lighter version was created that also included an S-shaped guard. This version of the kris, among others, was also used by the Katipuneros in their quest for independence.

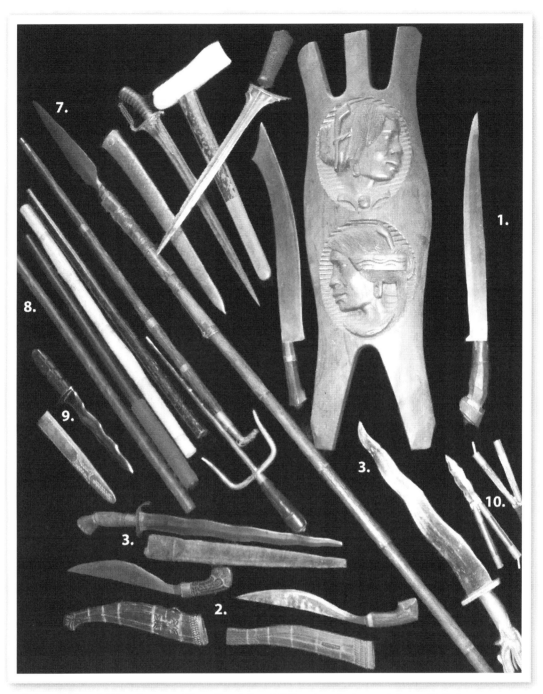

1. Bolo, 2. Talibon, 3. Kris, 4. Barong, 5. Kampilan, 6. Punal, 7. Bangkaw, 8. Garote, 9. Daga, 10. Balisong

Barong—Barongs have a finely forged leaf like blades with handles made of ivory, silver, gold or exotic woods in the shape of cockatoos. These blades are extremely light and fast for their size. Some even say that these blades have the ability to cut through the barrel of a Springfield rifle.

Kampilan—The kampilan is a two handed sword. They are also made with Philippine hardwood handles and cross guards, and can be found with finely watered blades with temper patterns reminiscent of the katana (Samurai) sword. The Kampilan is wide at the tip and narrows towards the guard. Due to its peculiar shape the scabbard was open on its side and the sword was held in place by a rattan or wicker binding. To unsheathe the sword all you have to do is strike.

Punal—The punal is a pistol grip push dagger. These daggers are finely made with nickel silver decoration on the guards and sheaths with exotic wood or ivory handles. These blades were designed for punching thrust movements.

Bangkaw—The bangkaw is a Philippine spear. It can have a rattan or hardwood shaft with a hand forged spear point in excess of 12 inches in length. The spear was a primary weapon in older styles that gave users the advantage of distance. Bangkaw can be found in single and double bladed versions.

Daga—The espada (dagger or knife) is an off-hand weapon that can be used alone or in conjunction with the stick or sword. Depending on its shape it can be used to stab or in slicing/cutting motions.

Balisong—The balisong is better known as the butterfly knife, or the Batangas knife. It is a fast opening knife with a blade incased between two handles. These knives come in single edge, double edge and kris edge.

What "Not to Do" with Bladed Weapons

The blocking and hitting of weapon edge to weapon edge will destroy the cutting edge on your swords or bolos. It is easy to forget, when practicing with dull training weapons that the sharp edge of an actual sword can be quite delicate. In battle it would not be a good thing to have your weapon damaged, broken or stuck in the blade of your opponent's weapon. Even small nicks and abrasions can directly affect the end result.

The "Right Way" to Defend with a Bladed Weapon

In order to prevent damage to your weapons, you block or parry with the flat or back side of your sword. This will prevent your edges from chipping and getting damaged. If you are using a double edged sword, you obviously would just use the flat side of the weapon.

CHAPTER 3

DEROBIO PRELIMINARIES

Basic Concepts

The basis of Derobio Escrima is built on deflecting and controlling movements and techniques. First and foremost, the most important aspect is the principal of "passing" the attacking blow, thus redirecting the energy of your attacker, while a countermove is employed from the outside. It is this basic idea that gives this art the ability to level the playing field, allowing you to defend yourself against attackers that may be larger and stronger than you. By redirecting the attacker's energy, instead of meeting it force to force, Derobio has proven itself to be an effective self-defense art for practitioners of all ages, genders and physical fitness levels.

That being said, as with anything, there are no absolutes. There may be times when you will need to adapt to the given situation and a "force to force" response is unavoidable. Even in this case, the passing techniques can seamlessly be integrated into these situations, giving you a wider range of responses and options.

Derobio Escrima emphasizes disarming techniques and defensive behavior rather than aggressive actions. Disarming and rendering an attacker incapable of further aggression is the primary goal.

Rank Structure

In the Pedoy style of Derobio Escrima, there are no belt rankings as are found in other traditional martial arts. Instead, there are four levels or shirt colors (white, black, blue, and red) which are then divided by four ranks within each color, with the exception of red which has six. As a student begins their journey in Derobio Escrima, they start by wearing a plain white tee-shirt and black pants. The right to wear the school uniform must be earned and is not given lightly. Shirt colors denote the following ranks:

White - Beginning Student
Black - Advanced Student
Blue - Assistant Instructor
Red - Full instructor

Gold / Yellow is worn only by the Grandmaster

It is important to note that rank shirts are not to be worn outside of class. While wearing your rank shirt your actions represent your instructor and your school. Always keep this in mind. Other "promotional" shirts can be purchased by students who wish to show off their school pride and help promote the art.

Training Overview

Derobio training begins with the basic exercises, the first 12 strikes and 12 defenses. The 12 strikes or Doce Teros are similar to many other Filipino martial arts. They are practiced on the instructor's count (in Spanish) and are continuous in movement. These strikes are practiced in a four corner pattern, striking all 12 angles then turning a quarter turn to the left (moving in a counter clockwise direction), and repeating to all four sides.

The 12 defenses are not blocks in the traditional sense; there is no force-to-force contact. Instead, opposing strikes are deflected or passed. The defenses are also practiced in a four corner pattern although the quarter turn is now to the right (moving in a clockwise direction).

Once the student has become proficient in these basic movements they are paired and they begin striking and defending alternately. These drills are done slowly at first but soon move to "real time" speed, allowing for automatic or reflexive actions to be ingrained into the student's subconscious behaviors.

Basic counters are quickly added to the defensive strikes which may include strikes to the wrist, elbow and collarbone. As the student progresses, more counters are added including knees, ankles, head strikes, punching, kicking, locks, disarms, takedowns and chokes.

Because of the efficiency of the Derobio system, locks and disarms become more accessible; that is, easier to do. Each counter has a series of locks, counter locks, counter-to-the-counter locks, disarms and tie-ups. These methods are practiced single stick to single stick, single stick to double stick, double stick to double stick, single stick to empty hand, double sticks to empty hand, and hand to hand. Derobio students work to cover as many situations as possible.

Double sticks or "doble cada" teaches the weaving stick motions of Sinawali, gunting or scissor blocks, following blocks, double stick attacks and, of course, disarms and locks. Sinawali (double stick weaving patterns) are learned not as individual sets but as a single exercise using different Siniwalli patterns, flowing one into the other with no pause. All double stick defenses are practiced in a flowing series against the 12 strikes. As the student becomes more proficient multiple counters are added as are disarms, locks and counter locks. At an advanced level these are practiced with live blades.

It is a common misconception that the art of Escrima is exclusively practiced with the famed Escrima sticks. Although the primary focus is on weapons, whether a stick, a bolo, pocket knife or any weapon available, it would be a severe underestimation to assume it ends there. Bone crushing kicking techniques are employed in combination with aggressive footwork, empty hand techniques, boxing, wrestling and groundwork skills. Basically, if it can be done with a weapon, it can be done without one.

Sparring drills can consist of padded stick sparring, live stick sparring with minimal gear, multiple attackers against one person (armed or unarmed). Any or all of the drills are practiced in standing and low point positions.

Four Stages of Development

The student of Derobio strives to reach the four stages of development: Physical, Mental, Moral and Spiritual. In the Physical Stage the student develops his balance, studies the 12 main body joints and learns to relax and flow fluidly from one movement to another. At this level he gains accuracy and control. Physical fitness and flexibility is improved in addition to a better understanding of the human body and its weaknesses/strengths.

The Mental Stage involves focus, improved learning skills, concentration and the ability to "read" the opponent. The mental level student moves beyond the physical lessons and the student begins to learn and understand history, terminology, and the cultural aspects and influences of the art.

In the Moral Stage of a student's education, a broader sense of the escrimador and it's true definition begins to surface. The student becomes more aware of his/her physical self, the world around them and how they relate to their family, friends and fellow students. As their physical and mental abilities grow, the need for violence, vengeance, or hate subside, thus creating a calming state of moral and ethical being.

The final stage is Spiritual fulfillment. Regardless of religious leanings or convictions, the spiritual level speaks to a very private and intimate relationship you have with your inner self, your deity and how you approach life. All classes are started and closed with a moment of silent prayer to encourage the student's relationship with their spiritual self.

Salutation Postures and Formalities

Derobio Escrima is a martial art originating in the Philippines. Most terminology used in class is derived from the Philippine or Spanish languages. As with any martial art the basic classroom rules apply and are primarily focused on respect for rank, dojo, history of the art and respect for fellow students.

When entering the classroom or dojo, please wait for the instructor or assistant instructor to welcome you with a salute.

At the Beginning of class, students line up in order of rank, with the highest rank in the front left corner to the lowest rank in the right back corner. The command "an-dam" is given. This is a signal for students to fall into ranks and assume the "ready" position.

An-Dam—This stance consists of standing at attention, feet should width apart. The weapon is held in both hands; the right hand is clenched around the weapon, palm facing out and the left hand is holding he weapon with fingers

Andam

Saludo Front

Saludo Side

pointing up, palm facing in (as if holding a cutting weapon). When the command "An-dam" is given, students repeat the command letting the instructor know that they are indeed ready and paying attention and begin class.

Saludo—The saludo (salute) in Derobio Escrima is done by stepping forward with your right leg while holding your weapon in front of you, cupping the bottom of the weapon. This signifies that no blood will be spilled, or "I come in peace." After the saludo, the student returns to the ready position and waits for the next command.

Am-Po

Pangaje

Am-Po—Am-po is a preparatory command given prior to your prayer. It is similar to the saludo position but instead of stepping forward with your right, you are now stepping back with your left leg. The weapon is held vertically in front of you. The reason for stepping back is that you do not step up to God, but rather humbly step back prior to bowing your head.

Pangaje—From the last position, you now bring your weapon over your heart, bow your head, and say a silent prayer. When done, you resume the an-dam position, letting the instructor know you are ready to begin.

Classroom Etiquette

Always show respect to your instructor, fellow students and to your school.

Come to class prepared, in uniform, and ready to learn.

When the instructor is talking or demonstrating, kneel or squat down allowing all students to see and hear the instruction.

Ask relevant questions when appropriate. Taking care not to interrupt the class.

When standing or sitting, never point your weapon to the ground. Show respect for your instructor and your weapon.

Do

Do not throw or kick your weapons. Respect and responsibility are important lessons. This weapon may save your or someone else's life someday and deserves to be treated with respect.

Do not drop your weapon in class. A loose grip can cost you your life. Always maintain control of your weapon. During disarm practice, make sure you are truly disarmed.

Do not hold onto your weapon "at all costs," If it means or leads to you getting trapped, let it go and move on.

Never rest your stick on the ground. This gesture is both disrespectful and has a deadly meaning behind it. Pointing your weapon to the ground during the saludo signifies a fight to the death in many regions of the Philippines. It is thought to represent the blood running down the blade.

Don't

"Don't be a monkey! Let go if you have to, for to be the monkey is to die."
—GGM Brauilio Pedoy

CHAPTER 4

DEROBIO BASICS

12 Basic Striking Angles

It is extremely important to keep in mind that ideally all strikes should be treated as if they were performed with a cutting weapon, which will not only impact but draw through the body. It is important not to stop your strike at the point of impact, but rather to treat each strike as if it were going through the intended target at point A and out at point B. All of this is done with alternating footwork, utilizing both male and female triangles.

Angle	Direction	Foot position	Target
Angle # 1 *	Right to Left in Downward angle	Right foot steps forward	Left collarbone - across the torso - exiting lower right ribcage
Angle # 2	Left to Right in downward angle	Left foot steps forward	Right Collarbone - across the torso - exiting lower left ribcage
Angle # 3	Right to left across the waist or midsection	Right foot steps forward	Targets could include elbow, rib cage, hip or abdominal area
Angle # 4	Left to Right across the waist or midsection	Left foot steps forward	Targets could include elbow, rib cage, hip or abdominal area
Angle # 5	Palm up thrust or stab to the midsection below the belly button	Right foot steps forward	Lower abdominal stab
Angle # 6 **	High palm up thrust to the upper right portion of the torso	Left foot steps forward	Right lung or brachial plexus tie in
Angle # 7	High palm down thrust to the upper left portion of the torso	Right foot steps forward	Heart or Left Brachial plexus tie in
Angle # 8 ***	Right to left in upward angle	Stay on Right foot forward	Left knee, sciatic nerve, groin
Angle # 9	Left to right in upward angle	Left foot steps forward	Right knee, sciatic nerve, groin
Angle # 10	Right to left in horizontal motion at head level	Right foot steps forward	Left temple, neck or general head area
Angle # 11	Left to right in horizontal motion at head level	Left foot steps forward	Right temple, neck or general head level
Angle # 12	Vertical strike through the center of the body at a downward angle	Right leg steps forward	Crown of head, face, torso

* The collarbone is the preferred target over the head because it has a much higher success ratio. The head can bob and weave out of the way while it is much more difficult to move the entire torso.

** When performing a high striking movement, the empty hand moves to a low protective position. This High-Low hand position is called "major Y menor" (major and Mminor).

*** When striking a number 8, do not change foot positions. Lift the leg out of the way of the striking angle and shuffle forward with your right foot lead.

Basic Striking Angles

Male and Female Triangle Stepping

While performing your basic footwork, keep knees bent, spine straight and weight fluid. You should be able to shift your weight from front foot to back foot almost imperceptibly, making movements and directional changes hard to predict and faster to apply. When striking to the lower body, bend at the knees, keeping your torso upright and guarded for the elevation change rather than bending at the waist and exposing your head to your opponent.

In applying the concept of triangle footwork, don't think of the triangle as a stagnant drawing on the floor but rather as a triangle that moves with you as you turn, shift and step.

The male triangle is used mostly in attacking but can also be used in defense to break your opponent's base (balance). Starting with feet shoulders width apart, step forward to the point of the triangle with either your left or right foot. The point of the triangle is typically directly in front of your target.

The female triangle is used primarily in defense, but can also add extra power to an attack. From a center point, you step out and to the side of your attacker allowing you to pass the blow and defend, exposing the unprotected flank of your foe. The female triangle is also used for multiple attackers as you consistently move to your left. Because most people are right handed, as you defend stepping to your left the multiple attackers will be stacked up and have to move around each other to continue their attack.

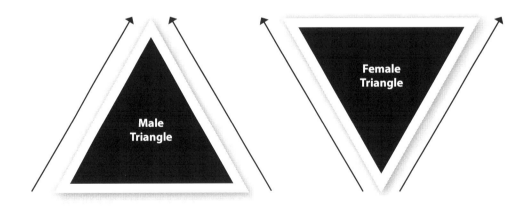

CHAPTER 5

DEROBIO ESCRIMA BASIC
DEFENSIVE METHODS

Basic Defenses Against the 12 Strikes

Defense Angle	Direction	Foot Position	Checking Hand Position
Angle # 1	Sweeping blow from left to right	Stepping with left foot	On elbow of striking hand or hard blow to shoulder *
Angle # 2	Sweeping blow from right to left	Stepping with right foot	On striking arm or empty hand of attacker
Angle # 3	Sweeping blow down from left to right	Stepping with left foot	On elbow or shoulder
Angle # 4	Sweeping blow down from right to left	Stepping with right foot	On empty hand or face of attacker
Angle # 5	Hit sharply down and to the right	Stepping with left foot	On weapon elbow or shoulder
Angle # 6	Holding stick slightly vertical, sweep right to left	Stepping with right foot	On empty hand, chest or inside of weapon arm
Angle # 7	Holding stick slightly vertical, sweep left to right	Stepping with left foot	Elbow of weapon hand, shoulder
Angle # 8	Sweeping left to right across lower legs	Stay on left foot, lift out of the way of strike	Elbow of weapon hand and shoulder
Angle # 9	Sweeping right to left across lower legs	Stepping with right foot	On empty hand, face, chest or inside of weapon arm
Angle # 10	Sweeping left to right deflecting blow over the head. Bend in the knees to lower stance	Stepping with the left foot	Elbow, shoulder
Angle # 11	Sweeping right to left deflecting blow over the head. Bend in the knees to lower stance	Stepping with the right foot	On empty hand, face, chest or inside of weapon arm
Angle # 12	Strike from left to right in a sharp upward angle deflecting blow	Stepping with the left foot	On Elbow, shoulder

*   In this series of photos the Author is seen grabbing the weapon hand. This is a more advanced type of check and should not be attempted by beginning students. Actually capturing and attacking blow is quite difficult. In the beginning, you'll find it much easier to think of the checking hand as a way to "push" your attacker away from you giving you more room to maneuver your weapon.

Basic Defense

Angle One

Angle Two

Angle Three

Angle Four

Basic Defense

Angle Five

Angle Six

Angle Seven

Angle Eight

Basic Defense

Angle Nine

Angle Ten

Angle Eleven

Angle Twelve

Use of the Checking Hand During Defense

The checking hand is used to interrupt the attacker's offense and defense. During offense, when you are the initiator of the attack, you can interrupt the defenders counter-defense just by using your checking hand to off-balance or even stop their blocks from coming out. Your checks can also be attacks to the central nervous system or internal organs.

In the Derobio defense, the use of the checking hand is used as a secondary defense/offense. For example, if you miss the block/parry, your checking hand should catch it. The checks should be performed with intensity. The check pulls, pushes, twists, grabs, pinches and hits. It is used to maneuver and disrupt your opponents body positioning.

As you can see in the photos above, the check is applied at or near the elbow. This is to prevent the elbow from being used as a counter. Photo 3 shows what is called the "C" hand and is a very destructive way of checking as it can cause hyper extension of the elbow.

Photo 4 shows the check redirecting a punch

Photo 5 shows the check being used to engage your opponent's non-weapon hand to keep him from countering and off balance. This could also be used as a standing body compression as you continue pushing forward and your hand causes his hand to hit his body, knocking the air out of him. Or, you can just skip to the face and perform a finger jab to the eyes.

Grabs are also an integral part of checks. Do not just grab for the sake of grabbing, always have a plan. Grabs can and will be used against you and vice-versa.

When grabbing, the meaty part of the thumb is the target. This gives you a solid place to start.

Photo shows the hand clamping down.

The thumb is placed on the opponent's pinky knuckle for leverage

This sequence of photos shows the use of the back of the hand in checking and grabbing. Photo 1 shows back of the hand to back of hand contact. Photo 2 shows the hand as it guides the hand away, photos 3 & 4 show the beginning of the thumb and stick grab. Photos 5 & 6 give you a closer view of hand positions. From here, you control the amount of pain to inflict.

Multiple Attacker Strategy

When dealing with multiple attackers, we must consider the type of strategy to use. Some people say go after the big guy first; others might tell you something totally different, like hit the closest one and so on. Well, you really need to understand why you do the things you do. Will they get you out of trouble, or get you into more trouble? Below I will give you a couple of scenarios, each designed to give you a little more insight into combative movement and its mind set.

1. If the biggest guy is in the center and you go after him, you can manage to do some damage but your victory will be short lived as this attack strategy will give ample time for the attackers on either side to come in around you. This will kill any and all chances of escape and really put a damper on your day.

2. Let's say that this time you go after the person to your right. This time all of the other attackers will come in right behind you, and again you're in trouble.

3. You now know that you should not attack to the center or to the right, because it puts you in danger of being overrun. So logically, this only leaves the left side. You might ask yourself why the left and not the right? Your opponents should be able to do the same thing and come in behind you, correct?

If you were defending force to force, then yes, this would be true. However, with the passing movements of Derobio, you will be able to position yourself to your advantage. What you have also to consider is that most attackers are right handed. Most likely, your attackers will be striking from right to left or if you're looking at the strike it's coming to the left side of your body. So in fact, by going after the attacker on your left, not only will you give yourself the opportunity to evade the

strike, you will also be lining up your opponents in a row, where they will have to go around each other to get to you. This also puts them in the path of the strikes that are headed your way and in danger of hitting themselves. You will further complicate their plans by redirecting all incoming strikes their way.

If the strike comes from their left or to your right side, just keep the strike going and still redirect it to your right. This strategy will slow them down, especially after one of them takes out one of their own. Always continue to redirect all strikes into oncoming opponents. This will create the time needed to make your counters work.

Remember don't do things because they look cool, do things because they work. Never cross in between your attackers, as this will give them your back. Look at everyone; never assume that a bystander will not take you out. Take the time to dissect everything you do and be fully aware of your environment.

CHAPTER 6

Derobio Escrima Basic Defensive Drills

Basic Three Defense

The "Basic Three Defense" is the first counter that is taught to all beginning students after they have an understanding of the strikes and blocks/parries. This sequence is used to teach the students targeting and more precise striking.

The targeted areas are the wrist, the elbow, and the wrist again, in this order. You are targeting the joints and learning how to check. That does not mean if another target becomes available and you hit it, that it's not good. All hits are good hits, but it is best to hit what you are aiming for.

Angle 1 — and all strikes coming from this side of the body

Stepping forward with your left foot, parry and check the weapon hand. Your check is used to put the target where you want it. Now hit the wrist with an Angle 1 strike. Come back up the same line with an Angle 9 strike, hit the elbow, and check before coming back down on the wrist again with an Angle 1 strike.

This is the same sequence that is used for angles 1, 3, 5, 7, 8*, 10, 12.

*Angle 8 keeps the same leg forward as in Angle 7, but you lift your leg up to avoid being hit and you do not give up any ground.

Angle 2 — and all strikes coming from the opposite side of the body

Stepping forward with the right foot, parry and check perform an Angle 2 strike down onto the wrist, check the left hand as you come up with an Angle 8 strike to the left elbow, and then strike back down again with an Angle 2 strike on the wrist.

This is the same sequence that is used for angles 2, 4, 6, 9, 11.

The amount of check you use can increase as your level of experience and mastery increases.

Basic Three
Angle #1

Basic Three
Angle #2

Basic Three
Angle #3

Basic Three
Angle #4

Basic Three
Angle #5

Basic Three
Angle #6

Basic Three
Angle #7

Basic Three
Angle #8

Basic Three
Angle #9

Basic Three
Angle #10

Basic Three
Angle #11

Basic Three
Angle #12

Little X Defense

The "Little X Defense" is the second defense taught to beginners. The main target areas are the wrist and the collar bone on both sides of the head. Similar to the Basic Three Defense, you step forward and parry, going with your opponent's force.

Angle 1 Little X Defense

After defending against an Angle 1 strike (and all strikes that are coming at the left side of your body—3, 5, 7, 8, 10, 12), check with your left hand, this is where you gauge and place your opponent's hand where you want it.

You now follow through with an Angle 1 strike to the wrist, immediately followed with Angle 2 and Angle 1 strikes to the collar bone. (Remember the reason we go to the collar bone is that if your opponent ducks or tries to evade they're actually putting their head in danger).

Angle 2 Little X Defense

The defense for Angle 2 (and all angles coming to your right side of your body—4, 6, 9, 11), starts by stepping forward with your right leg as you parry the Angle 1 strike to your left. Your checking hand helps with the parry.

You now perform an Angle 2 strike to the wrist while simultaneously checking your opponent's non-weapon hand, pushing it into his body to cause a standing compression that keeps your opponent off balance.

Follow up with an Angle 2 strike to the right collar bone and an Angle 1 strike to the left collar bone. This is a simple way of learning these defenses. Basically you are either defending the left side or the right side of your body. Remember, if it's too complicated to do in class it will be too complicated to do in the street while under pressure.

Little X Defense
Angle #1

Little X Defense
Angle #2

Little X Defense
Angle #3

Little X Defense
Angle #4

Little X Defense
Angle #5

Little X Defense
Angle #6

Little X Defense
Angle #7

Little X Defense
Angle #8

Little X Defense
Angle #9

Little X Defense
Angle #10

Little X Defense
Angle #11

Little X Defense
Angle #12

Big X Defense

The "Big X Defense" is multi-facetted in that it is both a defense and an offense. The Big X is used in other systems of Escrima in their offence or basic strikes. I sometimes call that the Big X with a period (stab). This we can perform in about ¾ of a second. Again let's start right off with the basic defense.

Angle 1 Big X Defense

After you defend against an Angle 1 strike and then check; you will counter with your own Angle 1 strike to the wrist as you pull your checking hand away. Next, you come up with an Angle 9 strike retracing the same line of Angle 1. This is followed by a palm-up check. The check will create an opening under the opponent's arms.

Now, execute an Angle 8 strike, which is performed by whipping your stick around and coming up under the exposed side of your opponent's weapon hand side. This is followed with an Angle 2 strike, which can be reinforced with your forearm or done on its own.

This defense is utilized against all attacks coming to the left side of your body: 3, 5, 7, 8, 10, 12.

Angle 2 Big X Defense

After defending against an Angle 2 strike, as shown previously, you counter with an Angle 2 strike to the wrist, followed immediately by whipping your stick around and coming up with an Angle 8 strike. This strike is aimed at the knees, but if you miss and hit the groin area, that is okay. This is followed by whipping your weapon around and coming up with an Angle 9 strike and a check to your opponent's hands, or with a standing body compression. The sequence ends with an Angle 1 strike to the collarbone, and due to where your weapon is this tends to be a power strike.

This defense is used against all attacks coming to the left side of your body: 4, 6, 9, 11.

Big X Defense
Angle #1

Big X Defense
Angle #2

Big X Defense
Angle #3

Big X Defense
Angle #4

Big X Defense
Angle #5

Big X Defense
Angle #6

Big X Defense
Angle #7

Big X Defense
Angle #8

Big X Defense
Angle #9

Big X Defense
Angle #10

Big X Defense
Angle #11

Big X Defense
Angle #12

Florete Defense

To correctly execute a "Florete (little flower) Defense," it is important to understand the components of it. One aspect is the abanico or "fanning" motion. The abanico can be performed to your front or to your side, and can be vertically, horizontally or some variation in between. This fan-like motion can be augmented or assisted by the Little X, or any other type of strike. In the following examples we will utilize the Little X.

Angle 1 Florete Defense

Use the Passing Defenses described on page 40 of the book. Parry the incoming strike in a left-to-right direction and check the weapon hand. Next, counter with an Angle 1 strike to the wrist followed by an abanico to the left and right sides of the temples. Finish with a Little X (Angles 1 & 2 strike combination) to both sides of the body. It could be aimed at the collarbone, the hands, or body. Again, like in the previous defenses, there is a left side and right side.

Angle 2 Florete Defense

Pass the Angle 2 strike from right to left followed by a left hand check. Your checking hand is your gauge; it lets you know exactly where your opponent's weapons hand is while you are concentrating on everything else. Counter with an Angle 2 strike to the opponent's weapon hand. Next, execute an Angle 1 strike to the collarbone followed by an abanico to the left and right sides of the temples. Simultaneously check the left hand or, if the hand is not there, a standing chest compression can be substituted. This combination is ended with Angle 1 & 2 strikes, and as you finish the combination a left hand strike to the neck can be applied.

Angle 3 Florete Defense

Deflect the incoming strike by hitting it down sharply. Counter strike the wrist with an Angle 1, followed by abanico strikes to both sides of the opponent's head. Simultaneously check the opponent's right arm, while you continue with Angle 1 and 2 follow up strikes. End this combination with a left-hand strike to the bridge of the opponent's nose.

Angle 4 Florete Defense

Hit the incoming strike down right to left in an arcing movement, making the opponent's strike miss you. Follow up with an Angle 2 counter strike to the opponent's weapon arm, while simultaneously checking your opponent's empty hand to prevent him from countering you. Follow this with an Angle 1 strike to eliminate both of his hands. Again follow with the abanico, this time striking the back of the head and the front of the face (do to the change in your opponent's body position). End the combination with Angle 1 and 2 strikes.

Angle 5 Florete Defense

Parry the stab and use a C-hand check to the opponent's elbow. Hit the hand with an Angle 1 strike followed by executing the abanico to both sides of the opponent's temple. End with Angle 1 and 2 strikes and a back forearm strike to the opponent's face.

Angle 6 Florete Defense

Parry the incoming strike from right to left and into your checking hand. Follow up with an Angle 2 strike to the opponent's weapon hand, and then an Angle 1 strike to the other hand. Continue your strikes with abanicos to both sides of the opponent's head, ending the combination with angles 1 and 2.

Angle 7 Florete Defense

Parry the strike from left to right using your left checking hand, being sure to control and place your opponent's weapon hand where you can hit it with an Angle 1 strike. Follow this with the abanico combination then end with strikes 1 and 2.

Angle 8 Florete Defense

Hit the incoming strike down to make it miss while simultaneously pulling your target leg out of the way. Counter with an Angle 1 strike followed by abanicos to both sides of the opponent's head. This can be performed while also slap-checking the face. End the combination with Angle 1 and 2 strikes.

Angle 9 Florete Defense

Hit the incoming strike down, from right to left, making the strike miss. Follow up with an Angle 2 counter strike to the opponent's weapon arm, while simultaneously checking your opponent's empty hand to prevent him from countering you. Follow this with an Angle 1 strike to eliminate both of the opponent's hands, and again follow with an abanico to both sides of the opponent's temple. End the combination with Angle 1 and 2 strikes.

Angle 10 Florete Defense

Parry the incoming strike from left to right, making the strike miss, while simultaneously ducking under it, and checking the opponent's weapon hand. Next, execute an Angle 1 strike to the opponent's wrist followed by an abanico to the left and right sides of the opponent's temples. Finish with a Little X or Angle 1 and 2 combination to both side of the opponent's body.

Angle 11 Florete Defense

Pass the strike from right to left while simultaneously ducking under it. Counter with an Angle 2 strike to the opponent's weapon hand. Next, execute an Angle 1 strike followed by an abanico to the left and right sides of the opponent's temples. Simultaneously check the opponent's left hand or, if the hand is not there, a face check can be substituted. This combination is ended with an Angle 1 and 2 strike combination.

Angle 12 Florete Defense

Parry from left to right using your left checking hand for control to place your opponent's weapon hand where you can hit it with an Angle 1 strike. Follow this with an abanico to the left and right sides of the opponent's temples. Be sure to use your checking hand to check your opponent's body position. This combination is ended with an Angle 1 and 2 strike combination.

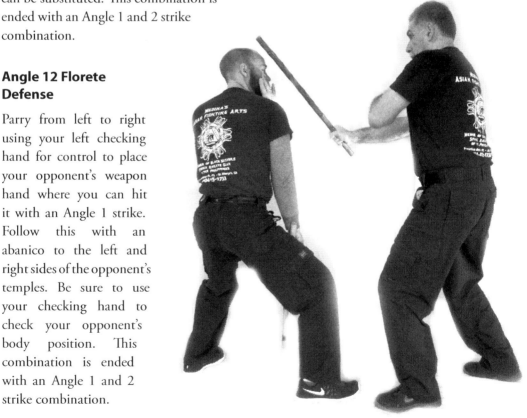

Florete Defense
Angle #1

Florete Defense
Angle #2

Florete Defense
Angle #3

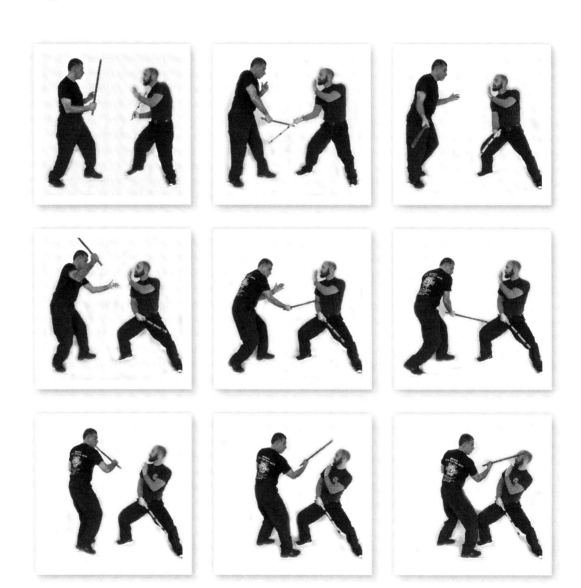

Florete Defense
Angle #4

Florete Defense
Angle #5

Florete Defense
Angle #6

Florete Defense
Angle #7

Florete Defense
Angle #8

Florete Defense
Angle #9

Florete Defense
Angle #10

Florete Defense
Angle #11

Florete Defense
Angle #12

CHAPTER 7

DEROBIO EMPTY HAND TECHNIQUES

"What happens if you don't have a stick?" This is one of the most commonly asked questions of Escrima practitioners. What most people don't realize is that all Escrima defenses and counters can be just as easily employed with the empty hands. In this chapter I will demonstrate the basics of these as done in Derobio Escrima.

Palm Up Knife Defense

I am showing this particular defense first because it was one of Grandmaster Pedoy's favorites. As the opponent's knife approaches you, point palm down (as in Angle 7) and insert your left hand palm up as shown. The fingers fan down and around to the left and then upward, while you simultaneously insert your right hand for a palm down grab. Roll the wrist towards your opponent to lock his joints, causing his head to go forward and down to meet either foot.

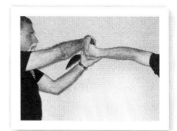
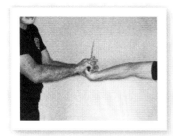

Defense Against a Hooking Knife Thrust

Intercept the incoming blow by pushing/hitting it downward and passing it to your right hand while at the same time hitting the opponent in the face with a left back-fist strike. This will occupy his non-weapon hand and give you time to spin right and bring his arm over your head to a position that will allow both of your hands to clamp down as you pull him hard to the floor. As your opponent's body slams the ground you drop your right knee down onto his floating ribs. This will create a body compression. As all the air is leaving the opponent's body you pull up on his arm to dislocate his elbow and possibly tear his shoulder.

  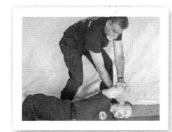

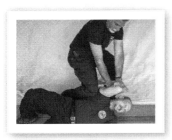

Defense Against a Backhand Knife Slash

The attacker starts with a left-to-right back hand strike. Move your left leg to a 45-degree angle so you are moving in the same direction as the oncoming strike. Hit the incoming strike with the back of your left hand to move it down and make it miss. Guide the strike to your right hand, snatching it with a palm down grab, and then roll your fingers forward. This should make your opponent want to reach for the floor as you kick between his legs.

Defense Against a Right Hand Punch (No. 1)

This technique is performed while standing right leg forward. Using both hands, one hand deflects while the other hand reaches out and grabs the opponent's fingers. Twist down and towards the attacker's armpit while at the same time grabbing his elbow for greater leverage.

View of the same technique as performed from the opposite side.

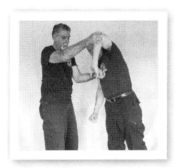

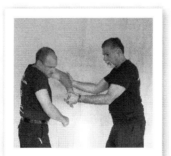
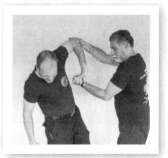

Defense Against a Right Hand Punch (No. 2)

Deflect the oncoming right-hand punch from the inside. Shuffle forward with your right leg as your right hand deflects the punch from right to left. Shoot forward with your right elbow to your opponent's face or solar plexus. This is followed by a chop to his carotid artery. Next, dig your fingers into the nerves along the back of the opponent's neck. This is all done while rotating the head to meet your oncoming knee strike. Continue to push the opponent's head under your armpit. As the opponent falls, follow him to the ground and, with your free hand, apply a wrist compression while simultaneously applying downward pressure on him with your knees.

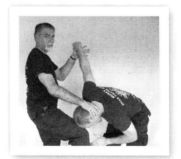

Defense Against a Right Hand Punch (No. 3)

Deflect the oncoming right-hand punch with your right hand as you rake the opponent's face and eyes with your left hand. Simultaneously, wrap your left hand around the opponent's elbow as you pivot to the right, causing a hyperextension of the opponent's arm. Reach out with both hands and grab the attacker's fingers and make a wish as you split them apart.

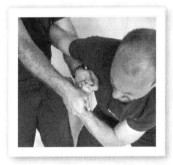

Defense Against a Right Hand Punch (No. 4)

While hitting the incoming punch down, simultaneously grab the attackers left hand-fingers, forcefully bend the fingers straight back and down. This will cause your opponent to drop to their knees. As they drop, your knee rises to meet them.

  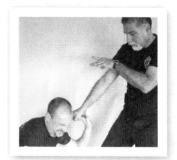

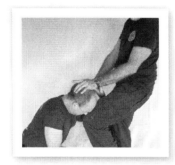

CHAPTER 8

INTRODUCTION TO DEROBIO
COUNTER LOCKS

Until recently, Derobio Escrima has been a relatively unknown martial art outside the Philippines and the Hawaiian Islands. The martial arts community has, with great respect, welcomed this newly discovered and extremely devastating art form. One of the many things that set this martial art apart from others is its counter-to -counter concept. Many martial arts, to some extent, have counters and locks that appear impossible to counter, but this is where the counter-to-counter locks of Derobio begin.

Derobio has taken this ability to new heights. Teaching the concepts of body structure, movement, and the chess-like prediction of the opponent's next move.
The art of Derobio has 144 counter locks which are unique to the system. The locks and counter locks in Derobio Escrima are very complex in their simplicity and work at medium to very close range. These locks are applied to the joints, tendons, muscles, nerves and pressure points, effectively shutting down the opponent's ability to think about anything but the pain.

This knowledge was generally reserved for the most advanced students due to the amount of experience and control needed to practice these methods. Until recently very few outside of our schools have seen these locks, much less known of their existence.

In the next few pages, I would like to show you just a few of the 144 counters unique to Derobio. Each one teaches a lesson beyond the obvious. You can learn step 1, 2, 3 and so on, but the real lesson is in why it works and how the body responds to it.

Counter to Counter Angle 1

Angle 1 is countered with a passing motion. Defender applies a snake that bites to the attacker's weapon hand, re-counters with his own Angle #1. This is then redirected into the crook of the opponent's elbow, while at the same time your elbow is brought up and forward over your opponent's forearm. Now apply downward pressure. This technique can be used as pain compliance or as a totally destructive technique that can cause tendon and ligament tears and joint dislocations.

Counter to Counter Angle 2

Angle 2 is countered with a passing motion from right to left, locking the opponent's weapon hand with your empty hand with a palm up lock. Defender counters with their own Angle 2 strike. This is where you shoot your left hand, palm down, like a snake at the approaching weapon. Now circle your opponent's weapon over your head and down in front of you. Release the weapon as you pin it under your right armpit, as you simultaneously shoot your left arm forward under your opponent's elbow causing a hyperextension or break, this happens as you reach for your opponent's hand and peel it off your hand. This is where a Z-lock is applied. Now insert your weapon under the opponent's arm and then apply downward pressure.

Counter to Counter Angle 3

Angle 3 is hit down and passed. As the opponent's weapon hand passes you apply a wrist lock. Here is where you go with the lock; don't fight it, go ahead and let your elbow ride upward. As you pass the Angle 3 strike that's aimed at your midsection with your left hand and guide it to the forward part of your weapon hand elbow. This will cause a temporary lock as you push forward with your body weight and elbow. Now grab your opponent's wrist and bend it back towards you and compress the wrist.

Counter to Counter Angle 4

Angle 4 is passed right to left while hitting the stick. The back of the hand is placed on the back of the attacker's hand as it goes by and a wrist lock is applied while counter striking with Angle 4. Here is where the re-counter takes place. With the back of your hand you perform a snake that bites while at the same time brining your elbow over, now you have a double lock.

Counter to Counter Angle 5

Angle 5 stab is parried to the right while applying a wrist lock, and counters with an Angle 5 while still holding the wrist lock. Attacker parries attack with his empty left hand and pins the counter under his arm. Reach for your weapon hand while causing an elbow break or hyperextension, peel the opponent's hand off your weapon hand by bringing down your elbow and apply your own lock and hits.

Counter to Counter Angle 6

Angle 6 is parried right to left and is countered with a wrist lock which is applied with the left hand. The defender re-counters with an Angle 6 strike. Duck right, then catch and apply a wrist lock of your own, while simultaneously rolling your right hand up and over to the left over your opponent's weapon arm. This will cause a temporary locking situation which will give just enough time to let go your opponent's weapon as you peel the grab off of your weapon hand which will cause both of your opponent's arms to be locked and placed in a breaking or hyper extension situation.

AFTERWORD

Photo Credit: Steve R. Leimberg

I hope you have enjoyed reading this book, trying the exciting techniques and applications described in its pages and, in the process, learned a little about the Philippine martial art of Derobio Escrima.

It has always been my desire to spread the knowledge bestowed upon me with all the love and excitement I have for this art. As one of my students once said, "When Master Medina teaches, he shares his knowledge so freely, it's like trying to take a sip of water from a Fire Hose!" I am truly happiest when I see the spark of learning in an eager student or hear the success stories told to me by people who were able to employ these methods in real life situations.

I have tried to acknowledge everyone but I too am getting older and if someone has slipped my mind, I do apologize.

Please be safe. When attempting these drills, wear the proper equipment and always practice restraint and control. And in the end, have fun, learn something new, respect something old, and become a better martial artist through growth and enlightenment.

TAMBULI MEDIA

Excellence in Mind-Body Health & Martial Arts Publishing

Welcome to Tambuli Media, publisher of quality books on mind-body martial arts and wellness presented in their cultural context.

Our Vision is to see quality books once again playing an integral role in the lives of people who pursue a journey of personal development, through the documentation and transmission of traditional knowledge of mind-body cultures.

Our Mission is to partner with the highest caliber subject-matter experts to bring you the highest quality books on important topics of health and martial arts that are in-depth, well-written, clearly illustrated and comprehensive.

Tambuli is the name of a native instrument in the Philippines fashioned from the horn of a carabao. The tambuli was blown and its sound signaled to villagers that a meeting with village elders was to be in session, or to announce the news of the day. It is hoped that Tambuli Media publications will "bring people together and disseminate the knowledge" to many.

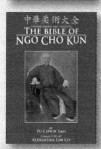

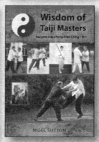

www.TambuliMedia.com

Printed in Great Britain
by Amazon